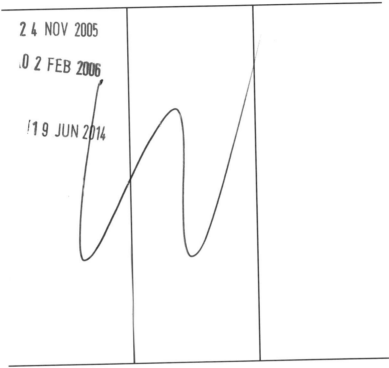

WELCOME TO MY COUNTRY

Welcome to
GREECE

FRANKLIN WATTS
LONDON·SYDNEY

This edition first published in 2005 by
Franklin Watts
96 Leonard Street
London EC2A 4XD

Franklin Watts Australia
45-51 Huntley Street
Alexandria NSW 2015

This edition is published for sale only in the United Kingdom & Eire.

© Marshall Cavendish International (Asia) Pte Ltd 2005
Originated and designed by Times Editions–Marshall Cavendish
an imprint of Marshall Cavendish International (Asia) Pte Ltd
A member of the Times Publishing Group
Times Centre, 1 New Industrial Road
Singapore 536196

Written by: Nicole Frank & Yeoh Hong Nam
Editor: Melvin Neo
Designer: Geoslyn Lim
Picture researcher: Susan Jane Manuel

A CIP catalogue record for this book
is available from the British Library.

ISBN 0 7496 6021 X

Printed in Singapore

PICTURE CREDITS
ANA Press Agency: 38
Giulio Andreini: 6, 18, 33 (bottom)
Archive Photos: 14, 17
Art Directors & TRIP Photographic Library:
    12, 22, 27, 33 (top), 39, 40
Camera Press: 15 (centre), 15 (bottom)
Bruce Coleman Collection: 3 (bottom),
    9 (bottom), 10
Sylvia Cordaiy Photo Library: 21, 23
Focus Team – Italy: 30, 41 (top)
Sonia Halliday: 32
Blaine Harrington: 4
HBL Network Photo Agency: 3 (centre), 5,
    7, 31 (top)
Dave G. Houser/Houserstock: 16, 31 (bottom)
The Hutchison Library: Cover, 1, 20, 24, 25, 34
The Image Bank: 41 (bottom)
Life File Photo Library: 28
North Wind Picture Archives: 15 (top), 29
Photobank Photolibrary: 3 (top), 26, 35
Pietro Scozzari: 2
Richard Shock/Silver Image Photo Agency: 43
David Simson: 37
Tom Till Photography: 8
Topham Picturepoint: 13, 19 (top), 36
Travel Ink: 9 (top), 11, 19 (bottom), 45

Digital Scanning by Superskill Graphics Pte Ltd

Contents

5 **Welcome to Greece!**

6 **The Land**

10 **History**

16 **Government and the Economy**

20 **People and Lifestyle**

28 **Language**

30 **Arts**

34 **Leisure**

40 **Food**

42 **Map**

44 **Quick Facts**

46 **Glossary**

47 **Books and Web Sites**

48 **Index**

Words that appear in the glossary are printed in **boldface** type the first time they occur in the text.

Welcome to Greece!

Although Greece may be known for its rocky terrain, the country actually boasts a wide variety of scenery. The Greek landscape features fertile river basins, dense forests and warm, sandy beaches. Let's learn all about Greece — its complex history, vibrant people and incredible culture!

Opposite: Greek soldiers dressed in traditional uniforms march at the Acropolis.

Below: Local women chat with tourists on the island of Kárpathos.

The Flag of Greece

The Greek flag consists of blue and white stripes with a white cross on the top left corner. Blue represents the sky and sea. White reflects Greece's fight for independence. The cross represents Greek Orthodox Christianity.

The Land

Greece, or the Hellenic Republic, sits on 130,800 square kilometres of land. Eighty per cent of the country is covered by mountains that run north-west to south-east. The sea cuts deep into the Greek mainland. Greece is bordered by Albania, the Former Yugoslav Republic of Macedonia, Bulgaria and Turkey.

Below: The island of Crete is home to golden beaches and blue-green seas.

Left: Located in the Aegean Sea, Santorini consists of five islands. They were created about four thousand years ago in a violent volcanic eruption.

Islands and Volcanoes

The valleys and mountains of Greece were formed between 65 million and 1.7 million years ago. During this time, volcanic eruptions also created many new islands.

Today, Greece consists of three parts: the northern mainland which connects Greece to the rest of Europe; the southern mainland; and the islands and archipelagos. The islands occupy 18 per cent of the Greek territory.

Climate

Greece has a mild climate. Mountains in the north attract rain, and sea breezes make the coastal sun pleasant. Average summer temperatures hover around 27° Celsius (C) but heat waves occasionally bake the country.

Winters in Greece are wet, but the temperature rarely dips below 6°C. Mountains are capped with winter snow until spring.

Above: Delicate, yellow wildflowers blossom in front of rocks formed during a volcanic eruption many centuries ago.

Plants and Animals

Many types of trees and flowers, such as oaks, pines, firs, tulips and irises, flourish in Greece. Some plants have developed into unique species.

Various animals, such as wildcats, deer and jackals, make their home in Greece. Birds from northern Europe fly to Greece to escape the cold of winter.

Above: These purple bellflowers add a patch of colour to the rocky slopes of Mt. Parnassus. Plants in Greece have adapted to the dry soil by growing fewer leaves and becoming shorter than similar plants in other countries.

Left: This rare lynx, a type of wildcat, perches on a rock to survey its territory.

9

History

Greek history dates back nearly four thousand years when the Minoan civilisation was established in Crete. Through the centuries, the Greek navy and army sailed the Mediterranean Sea and invaded areas as far north as modern Russia.

During the fifth century B.C., Greece consisted of city-states. In 500 B.C., the Greek city-states defeated the Persians, who came from the Middle East.

Below: Tourists visit the ancient ruins of the Minoan palace of Knossos in Crete.

Macedonia and Byzantium

Around 350 B.C., King Philip II of Macedonia conquered the Greek city-states. His son, Alexander the Great, united Greece and expanded Greek civilisation into Egypt, northern India and Persian territories. In 146 B.C., Greece became part of the Roman Empire. When the empire split in two in A.D. 285, Greece became part of the eastern half of the Byzantine Empire and Constantinople became its capital.

Above: An ancient Ionic column (*in the foreground*) and a Byzantine church (*in the middle*) blend into the architecture of modern Athens.

Left: A colourful tapestry shows the Turks' surrender in the Greek war of independence, which lasted from 1821 to 1829.

Independence and War

The Byzantine Empire was divided in the thirteenth century. In 1453, Constantinople fell to the Turkish-ruled Ottoman Empire. After centuries of **oppression**, the Greeks rebelled in 1821 and the Turks eventually granted Greece its independence in 1829.

In 1831, the first Greek president was **assassinated**, and **civil war** erupted. Many changes in government followed. In 1912, Italy attacked the Ottoman Empire and Greece seized many important territories from Turkey.

Greece participated in World War I (1914–1918) but failed to gain new territory. Italy and Germany invaded Greece during World War II (1939–1945), but Greece resisted and eventually defeated these powers.

Below: In 1941, German and Italian soldiers prepare for a victory parade in Athens.

Democracy Once More

The defeated German troops left Greece in 1945. Civil war loomed as the communists struggled for power. From 1949 to 1969, the United States of America provided Greece with money and arms to fight **communism**.

In 1967, the Greek military formed a **junta** called "the colonels". In 1974, the junta collapsed and Konstantinos Karamanlis began restoring democracy.

Below: Konstantinos Karamanlis (1907–1998) was Greece's prime minister from 1955 to 1963 and again from 1974 to 1980. He was influential in Greek politics during the 1970s and 1980s and was elected president in 1980 and 1990.

Solon (c. 630–530 B.C.)

Solon was the Athenian statesman who abolished slavery in Athens. He struggled for humane laws and fought against poverty. Solon was one of the Seven Wise Men of Greece.

Solon

Andreas Papandreou (1919–1996)

Andreas Papandreou left Greece when the colonels took power but later returned and founded the Panhellenic Socialist Movement (PASOK). In 1981, he was elected prime minister. He retired from politics in 1996.

Andreas Papandreou

Melina Mercouri (1925–1994)

The arts scene flourished under Melina Mercouri, the minister of culture appointed in 1981. She is best known for asking Britain to return the Elgin Marbles to Greece, sculptures once removed from the Parthenon.

Melina Mercouri

Government and the Economy

Government

Greece is a presidential republic. The basis for the current Greek constitution was formed when the colonels fell in 1974. The president is elected by the parliament to a five-year term and he or she has only ceremonial powers. The *vouli*, or parliament, and the prime

Below:
The parliament building looks out over Constitution Square in Athens.

minister hold real power. The vouli
consists of 300 members who are
elected to four-year terms by ballot.

Greece has 13 regions, divided
into 51 prefectures. The two major
political parties are the Panhellenic
Socialist Movement and the New
Democratic Party.

Six per cent of Greece's national
budget is spent on defence. Greek
men must serve in the military.

Economy

Greece has made economic progress in recent years but it still falls behind other European Union (EU) countries. Shipping and tourism are Greece's main sources of income.

Historically, most Greeks prefer to be self-employed than to work for big companies. Greece's service industry now generates 60 per cent of the national income. Today, fewer Greeks leave to work overseas.

Above:
Green grapes are harvested in Crete. A large variety of fruit is grown in Greece. This produce is sold locally and around the world.

Natural Resources

Fertile soil in Thessaly and in Eastern Macedonia and Thrace makes these regions important agricultural areas. Major crops include tomatoes, grain, sugar, cotton, olives, grapes, melons, oranges and peaches. In recent years, the fishing industry has declined.

Food, steel, cement and livestock are Greece's major exports. Greece trades mainly with other EU countries, especially Germany and Italy.

Above: Greek women examine containers of olives at a shop.

Left: Vehicles unload from a ship at the port of Preveza in Epirus. Shipping is an important part of the Greek economy.

People and Lifestyle

The Hellenes

Greeks, who call themselves Hellenes, have preserved their language, culture and identity, despite past invasions.

Today, Greece has a **homogeneous** population, with only 2 per cent being **ethnic minorities**. Ninety-eight per cent of the people belong to the Greek Orthodox Church.

Below: Two Greek children spend a day with their grandfather.

Above:
This shopkeeper
plays the guitar
while waiting for
customers.

Muslims and Albanians

Muslims make up about 1 per cent of the population and live in north-eastern Greece. They are represented by at least four parliament members.

Albanians were brought into Greece to settle in underpopulated areas in the 1100s. Today, their descendants consider themselves Greek. Recently, 300,000 Albanian refugees came to Greece and were given shelter and jobs.

Family

Greek families are close-knit. In the past, rural communities were very close because travel between villages was difficult. People living in cities tend to be more independent, but family life remains a top priority.

In the past, Greek families gave their marrying daughters **dowries** to ensure that the newly-weds had a

comfortable life. Today, this system is no longer practised. The government abolished the practice in the early 1980s, and many women are now financially independent. Today, Greek women are free to choose whether to have a job, a family or both.

Greek children are given two godparents, or ***nonos***, at birth. Godparents are responsible for a child's spiritual life and often also give financial and emotional support.

Education

Ancient Greece produced many famous thinkers. Education is still a priority today. From the ages of six to twelve, children attend primary school. They then spend three years at lower secondary school or *gymnasium*. Upper secondary school or *lyceum* follows.

Public education is free, but many students take additional classes at private schools.

Above: Students at this Greek primary school are eager to answer the teacher's question.

Further Education

Competition to enter a university is tough because schools are few in number. Today, secure jobs in the city, which often require university diplomas, attract many young people from the countryside.

The government has addressed its education shortage by improving schools and building new universities. Many students also participate in foreign exchange programmes.

Below: These university students stop to chat between classes.

Religion

In 1850, the Greek Orthodox Church became independent of Constantinople. Although the Church is self-governed, it recognises the Ecumenical Patriarch in Istanbul as its spiritual leader.

Ten million Greeks belong to the Church. Greece is divided into 81 dioceses, or religious districts, run by Orthodox bishops. Orthodox priests are active in community life and take part in many religious ceremonies.

Above: This abbot (*centre*) takes part in the **Niptras** before Good Friday. At this ceremony, priests re-enact Jesus Christ's washing of his disciples' feet before the Last Supper.

Greek Muslims, Roman Catholics, Protestants and Jews account for only 2 per cent of the Greek population.

Monasteries

Monasteries have helped shape Greek spiritual life for about 1,000 years. Some monks live secluded lives, while others are part of communities. Today, fewer and fewer people choose the monastic life.

Below: The isolated Meteora monasteries sit high atop the Pindus Mountains in Thessaly.

Language

Talk to Me

Greek, in one form or another, has been used for more than 3,000 years. It was the language of the Gospels and has contributed to all Western languages. In the third century, *dimotiki* was the spoken Greek dialect. In the 1830s, a new language called *katharévousa* was created. However, it was very hard to learn and in 1975, dimotiki became the official language.

Below: Both Greek and English are used on signs in Athens.

28

Left: This illustration depicts a scene from the life of Helen of Troy. The Trojan War between the Greeks and the city of Troy was recorded in Homer's *Iliad*.

A Good Story

Homer, a Greek poet, wrote the *Iliad*, one of the world's most famous ancient stories. It recounts the war between the Greeks and the city of Troy. Other famous ancient Greek writers include Sophocles and Euripides.

Modern Greek writers George Seferis and Odysseus Elytis won the Nobel Prize for literature in 1963 and 1979 respectively. Another modern Greek author, Níkos Kazantzakís, had two of his novels made into films.

Arts

Art through the Ages

Greek art has inspired the world for centuries. Builders in the geometric period (1100–700 B.C.) favoured simple lines. Temple ruins in Crete and Sparta are examples of this architectural style.

During the archaic period (700–500 B.C.), Greeks incorporated Egyptian stone columns and carvings into their

Below: Ancient Greeks visited the temple of Delphi to consult the **Oracle** of Apollo on private and political matters.

Left: Local store fronts display Greek handicrafts such as leather sandals, bags and rugs.

work. Human figures began to look more lifelike. Marble became a favoured building material during this period.

During the classical period (500–323 B.C.), the Greek city-states tried to outdo each other, building temples in the Doric, Ionic and Corinthian architectural styles.

Builders used elements of Asian art and architecture during the Hellenistic period (from 323 B.C.).

Below: This colourful vase is a **replica** of an ancient art treasure.

From Icons to Landscapes

Only fragments of early paintings survive, but religious icons from the Byzantine period have been preserved. Many icons depict Jesus Christ or the Virgin Mary with the infant Jesus. From the fifteenth to the nineteenth centuries, Italian Renaissance art influenced artists on the Ionian Islands. Modern Greek paintings depict landscapes and people.

Above: Biblical characters painted during the twelfth century decorate the walls of a church in Cyprus.

Opposite: Plays have been staged at the Theatre of Dionysus in Athens since the fifth century B.C.

All the World is a Stage

Classical Greek drama was not just entertaining, it also gave the audience a moral lesson. Both comedies and dramas demonstrated the beliefs and values of Greek society. Greek drama has greatly influenced many famous writers such as William Shakespeare.

Above: Traditional Greek actors wear stylised masks during dramatic productions.

During the classical period, plays were staged in open-air amphitheatres, where actors wore masks. Excellent **acoustics** allowed those sitting far away to hear the actors perfectly.

Leisure

Greece's warm climate lets people enjoy the outdoors throughout the year. City dwellers participate in exercise, go to parks and walk their dogs. Greek children enjoy card games and football.

In rural areas, people visit each other and host parties. Women make handicrafts which they hang in their sitting rooms. Other popular pastimes include sculpture, reading and writing.

Left: Boys play a game of cards in Cyprus.

Let's Celebrate!

Music, singing and dancing are popular
activities at Greek celebrations,
especially at Easter and Christmas.
Guitarists and drummers play lively
music, and people sing folk songs at
every occasion. Colourfully dressed
dancers also perform during festivals.
Greek folk dances range from the festive
and happy to the serious and solemn.

Above: Greek folk
dancers perform at
a festival.

Left: Cyprus football player Neophytus Larkou (*right*) vies for the ball in a 1993 World Cup qualifying match.

Sports

The prestigious Olympic Games began in ancient Greece. In 2004, the Olympic Games returned to Athens. Today, the country is home to amateur and professional athletes. Greek competitors in both wrestling and sailing have won Olympic medals.

Podosphero, or football, is Greece's national sport. The 18-team Greek football league plays games on Sunday and excited spectators fill the stands to watch. The Greek national team won the Euro 2004 football tournament despite being the underdog.

The Great Outdoors

Greeks love to relax in the great outdoors. Skiing, hunting and car racing are all popular pastimes. The clear blue waters of the Greek islands attract locals and tourists alike. These islands provide a perfect setting for water sports including fishing, sailing, boating and waterskiing. The clear waters also let swimmers and divers observe marine life.

Left:
Fresh lobsters are served to tourists at a seaside restaurant in Kérkira.

Holidays

Pascha, or Easter, is the most important day in the Greek Orthodox calendar. The carnival season takes place during the three weeks before Lent. On Holy Saturday, processions leave churches at midnight to re-enact the search for Christ's body. Dressed in their finest clothes, people feast and have fun after attending church on Easter Sunday.

Below: During Easter, women on the island of Kárpathos wear colourful, traditional dress with necklaces of gold coins to symbolise wealth.

Independence Day, celebrated on 25 March, marks the end of 400 years of Turkish rule in Greece. Greece eventually gained independence in 1829 after an eight-year war.

During World War II, Greek prime minister Ioánnis Metaxas replied, "*Ochi*," or "No," when Italy asked to occupy Greece. Ochi Day on 28 October celebrates Greek pride.

Above: Students and soldiers march through the streets on Ochi Day.

Food

The first cookbook in history was written in 330 B.C. by Greek Archestratos. Today, Greek cuisine has adopted ideas and flavours from the Middle East and Western Europe.

Simplicity, fresh ingredients, herbs and spices, and olive oil form the basis of good Greek food. Vegetables are

Below: An Easter Sunday feast is a good opportunity for the members of a large Greek family to get together.

fresh and tasty because Greece's sunny Mediterranean climate is very suitable for growing herbs and vegetables.

Greeks love seafood and lamb. Favourite dishes include *kalamari*, or squid, and *souvlaki*, or barbecued lamb kebabs. Fresh fruit and pastries are popular desserts.

Food and **hospitality** are important to Greek culture. Good cooks are well respected by friends and family.

A **B** **C** **D**

1

2

3

4

5

BULGARIA

F. Y. R.
MACEDONIA

EASTERN
MACEDONIA & THRACE

Istanbul
(Constantinople)

ALBANIA

CENTRAL
MACEDONIA

WESTERN
MACEDONIA

● Thessalon ki

PINDUS

Aliákmon

▲ Mount Olympus
(2,917 metres)

NORTHERN
AEGEAN

Piniós

EPIRUS

THESSALY

MTS

Akhelóös

TURKEY

IONIAN
ISLANDS

AEGEAN SEA

CENTRAL
GREECE

WESTERN
GREECE

Delphi ●

Mount
Parnassus
(2,457 metres)

▲

ATTICA

■ ATHENS

Olympia ●

Mykonos

CYCLADES
ISLANDS

PELOPONNESUS

MEDITERRANEAN SEA

● Sparta

SOUTHERN AEGEAN

Santorini

Kárpathos

Knossos ●

CRETE

GREECE

N
↑

42

Above: Boats cruise in a lake on one of the Santorini islands.

Aegean Sea C3
Akhelóös River A3
Albania A2
Aliákmon River B2
Athens B3
Attica B3

Bulgaria C1

Central Greece B3
Central Macedonia B2
Crete C5
Cyclades Islands C4

Delphi B3

Eastern Macedonia & Thrace C2
Epirus A3

Former Yugoslav Republic of Macedonia B1

Ionian Islands A3
Istanbul (Constantinople) D2

Kárpathos D5
Knossos C5

Mediterranean Sea A4-D5
Mount Olympus B2
Mount Parnassus B3
Mykonos C4

Northern Aegean C3

Olympia B4

Peloponnesus B4
Pindus Mountains A2-B3
Piniós River B3

Santorini C4
Southern Aegean C4

Sparta B4

Thessaloníki B2
Thessaly B3
Turkey D3

Western Greece A3–B3
Western Macedonia A2–B2

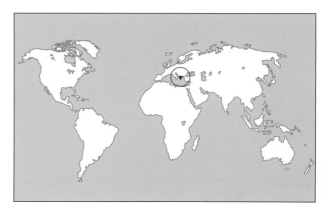

Quick Facts

Official Name	The Hellenic Republic
Capital	Athens
Official Language	Greek
Population	10,647,529 (July 2004 estimate)
Land Area	130,800 square kilometres
Regions	Attica, Central Greece, Central Macedonia, Crete, Eastern Macedonia and Thrace, Epirus, Ionian Islands, Northern Aegean, Peloponnesus, Southern Aegean, Thessaly, Western Greece, Western Macedonia
Highest Point	Mount Olympus (2,917 metres)
Major Rivers	Aliákmon, Akhelöós, Piniós
Official Religion	Greek Orthodox Christianity
Famous Leaders	Alexander the Great
	Elefthérios Venizélos
	Constantine Karamanlis
	Andreas Papandreou
Important Holidays	Pascha, or Easter; Independence Day; Ochi Day
Currency	Euro (EUR 1.515 = £1 as at July 2004)

Opposite: The island of Mykonos has an unusual mascot — Petros the pelican!

Glossary

acoustics: the features of a room or theatre that determine how clearly sounds are heard in it.

assassinated: murdered for political or religious reasons.

civil war: a war between two groups from the same country.

communism: a system of government based on the common ownership of property.

dimotiki: demotic Greek, a commonly spoken form of the Greek language.

dowries: the items a woman brings to her husband when she gets married.

ethnic minorities: racial or national groups that make up small parts of the population.

gymnasium: a secondary school for young people aged thirteen to fifteen.

homogeneous: all of the same kind.

hospitality: being nice and welcoming to guests in your home.

junta: a small group ruling a country, especially after a coup and before a legal government has been instituted.

kalamari: squid.

katharévousa: "pure" Greek, a form of Greek that is close to ancient Greek.

lyceum: an institution that students attend from age sixteen.

Niptras: the washing ceremony before Good Friday that re-enacts Jesus Christ's washing of his disciples' feet before the Last Supper.

nonos: a godparent.

ochi: no.

oppression: the state of being subdued and kept down through harsh and cruel use of power or authority.

oracle: a shrine or temple at which requests are made to a deity (god) and divine answers conveyed through a medium or priest.

Pascha: Easter.

podosphero: football.

replica: a copy or duplicate.

souvlaki: grilled or barbecued pieces of lamb on skewers.

vouli: the Greek parliament.

More Books to Read

Alexander the Great. Famous Lives series. Jane Bingham (Usbourne Publishing Ltd)

Ancient Greeks. Focus on the Ancient World series. Anita Ganeri (Franklin Watts)

Everyday Life in Ancient Greece. Clues to the Past series. A. Pearson (Franklin Watts)

Greece. A Visit to series. Peter Roop, Connie Roop (Heinemann Library)

Greece. The Changing Face Of series. Tamsin Osler (Hodder Wayland)

The Groovy Greeks. Horrible Histories series. Terry Deary (Scholastic Hippo)

In the Daily Life of the Ancient Greeks. Gods and Goddesses series.
    Fiona MacDonald (Hodder Wayland)

Videos

Ancient Greece – A Journey Back in Time. (Cromwell Productions)

Web Sites

www.ancientgreece.com

www.bbc.co.uk/schools/ancientgreece/main_menu.shtml

www.gogreece.com/learn/history/Byzantine_empire.html

www.perseus.tufts.edu/Olympics/

Due to the dynamic nature of the Internet, some web sites stay current longer than others. To find additional web sites, use a reliable search engine with one or more of the following keywords to help you locate information about Greece. Keywords: *Alexander the Great, Athens, Cyprus, Olympic Games, Parthenon, Z·kinthos.*

Note to parents and teachers
Every effort has been made by the Publishers to ensure that these web sites are suitable for children, that they are of the highest educational value, and that they contain no inappropriate or offensive material. However, because of the nature of the Internet, it is impossible to guarantee that the contents of these sites will not be altered. We strongly advise that Internet access is supervised by a responsible adult.

Index

agriculture 19
Albanians 21
Alexander the Great 11
animals 9
architecture 11, 30, 31
art 15, 30, 31, 32
Athens 11, 13, 15, 16,
    28, 32

beaches 5, 6
Byzantine Empire 11, 12

children 24, 34
Christmas 22, 35
climate 8, 34, 41
colonels, the 14, 15, 16
communism 14
Constantinople 11,
    12, 26
Crete 6, 10, 18, 30
culture 5, 15, 20, 41

democracy 14, 17
dimotiki 28

economy 16, 18, 19
education 24, 25
ethnic minorities 20

family 22, 40, 41
festivals 35
folk dances 35

food 18, 19, 37, 40, 41

government 16, 23, 25
Greek Orthodox Church
    5, 20, 26, 27, 38

handicrafts 31, 34
Hellenistic period 31
history 10–15

Iliad 29
independence 5, 12,
    13, 39
Independence Day 39

Karamanlis, Konstantinos
    14
Kárpathos 5, 38
katharévousa 28

language 20, 28

Mercouri, Melina 15
Metaxas, Ioánnis 39
military 14, 17
Minoan civilization 10
monasteries 27
music 35
Muslims 21, 27

Niptras 26

nonos 23

Ochi Day 39
Olympic Games 36
Oracle of Apollo 30
Ottoman Empire 12, 13
outdoors 34, 37

Papandreou, Andreas 15
Parthenon 15
Pascha 38
pastimes 34, 37
plants 9
podosphero 36

religion 5, 26
rural communities 22

temples 30, 31
tourism 10, 18, 37
Turkish rule 12, 39

United States 14
universities 25

volcanoes 7, 8
vouli 16

women 23
World War I 13
World War II 13, 39